MW01005334

DISCIPLINE IN SCHOOL-AGE CARE
Control the Climate, Not the Children

by
Dale Borman Fink

School-Age NOTES
P.O. Box 40205 ● Nashville, TN 37204

Discipline in School-Age Care: Control the Climate, Not the Children, was originally written as a paper for the ***Issues in School-Age Child Care*** series produced by **LATCHKEY Services for Children, Inc.**, Clearwater, FL. The original title of the publication was "Behavior Management."

Illustrations by: Julie Sorensen

10   9   8   7   6   5   4   3   2   1

ISBN: 0-917505-07-7

© Copyright 1995, 2004. **Dale Borman Fink**
All Rights Reserved.
Published by: School-Age NOTES
                P.O. Box 40205
                Nashville, TN 37204

Table of Contents

About the Author

Dale Borman Fink, Ph.D. is one of the most widely recognized authors and public speakers associated with the field of school age care. He has been a keynote speaker across the United States as well as in Canada and Australia.

Among his publications have been School-Age Children With Special Needs: What Do They Do When School Is Out? (1988, Boston: The Exceptional Parent Press) and Making a Place for Kids with Disabilities, (2000, Praeger Publishers, Westport, CT).

Dr. Fink spent 12 years on the front lines of child care as a teacher and administrator in both preschool child care and school age care, followed by eight years at the Center for Research on Women at Wellesley College in Massachusetts, doing writing, training, and research.

Dr. Fink received his B.A. from Harvard in 1972 and a Ph.D. in special education from the University of Illinois at Urbana-Champaign in 1997. He currently holds a part-time faculty appointment with the University of Connecticut Center for Excellence in Developmental Disabilities, and spends the balance of his time as an independent scholar and consultant. He resides with his wife and son in Williamstown, Massachusetts.

For more information or to contact Dr. Fink, visit his website, www.includeallkids.com.

Introduction

> *"Put twenty or more children of roughly the same age in a little room, confine them to desks, make them sit in lines, make them behave. It is as if a secret committee, now lost to history, had made a study of children and, having figured out what the greatest number were least disposed to do, declared that all of them should do it."*

This quotation from the book *Among Schoolchildren* by Tracy Kidder (1989, Boston: Houghton-Mifflin, p. 115) provides a good starting point for thinking about the management of children's behavior in school-age care settings. All the children who attend school-age care (SAC) also attend school. SAC is designed to serve them during the days and hours when school classrooms are not in session. It is useful, therefore, to think about what they are experiencing during those many days and hours *inside* the classroom, before and after they attend our programs. Kidder was exaggerating. Nevertheless, his description has a ring of truth. For better or for worse, the daily experience of millions of school children continues to reflect the dictates of this "secret committee." Even the most nurturing classroom may require children to spend much of their time doing what they are "least disposed to do."

Then they come to the school-age program. Are we obliged to continue the same patterns already established in the school classroom? Should teachers and caregivers in SAC settings follow the dictates of that same "secret committee"? Or should we offer something different, given that our goals and purposes differ from those of classroom teachers?

1

The Words We Use

Consider the words that are most frequently used to discuss the management of children's behavior: **behavior management.** Invariably this phrase is used when the subject is children's *misbehavior.* Yet the phrase isn't *misbehavior management,* is it? This book will help you see that the focus on *misbehavior* is part of the problem. You will have fewer problems with *misbehavior* if you place your focus on the positive, i.e., how to generate appropriate behavior. Furthermore, the word *management* in the phrase **behavior management** tends to get overlooked. The upcoming discussion will convince you that the way SAC directors, teachers and caregivers *manage* a program setting has everything to do with the type of behavior that is produced.

Consider another term: **discipline.** What does it mean -- and what do people mean when they say that children need more of it? Does it mean *intimidation?* Does it mean "yours is not to reason why, yours is but to do or die"? Does it mean waiting patiently and quietly, even if you have nothing to do and you are only six- years-old? **Discipline** contains the word *disciple.* A *disciple* is a willing follower, someone who is happy to respond to your requests and demands because you have won that person's trust and confidence. If you obtain children's compliance through bribery, threats or intimidation, then they are not your disciples. The discussion that follows will help you cultivate disciples.

2

"Through The Back Door" . . . Suppose You Wanted To Promote Misbehavior!

Sometimes it is possible to gain insights into a subject by coming at it "through the back door." For instance, if you wanted to have fewer weeds in your garden, you might try to imagine all the things you could do to *encourage* the growth of weeds. You would then set out to make sure you were *not* doing those things. Let's try something similar with behavior among children in a SAC setting.

Try this exercise:
Imagine, for a few minutes, that your goal was to *encourage* as much *inappropriate behavior* as possible. What could you do to accomplish that goal?

➤ Write down some of your ideas on a piece of paper now. Be imaginative! Don't hold yourself back.

➤ Read further to see some ideas generated by school-age care staff who have engaged in this imaginative exercise in workshops on this subject.

3

How To Promote *Mis*behavior In SAC
(Ideas generated by workshop participants)

1. Confuse the children about the rules -- don't post any and don't explain them either.

2. Set up the room in such a way that traffic patterns encourage confusion and conflict.

3. Allow staff to preoccupy themselves with personal telephone calls, talking to parents and each other.

4. Provide very few activities -- and only the same ones the children have seen a hundred times before.

5. Require the youngest children to maintain their concentration as long as the oldest are capable.

6. Require the oldest to do activities designed with the youngest in mind.

7. Require all children to remain in groups by grade level regardless if they would like to play with older or younger friends.

8. Do things for the children that they are capable of doing for themselves -- such as pouring juice or milk. Don't let them take on any responsibilities.

9. Provide only negative ("don't!") directions, not positives.

10. Keep the environment unattractive, cluttered and disorganized.

(*Exercise, cont.*)

11. Limit the amount of snack food so children are feeling hungry and frustrated when snack time has ended.

12. Provide furniture which is uncomfortable and chairs that are the wrong size for the children.

13. Provide no positive individual attention or affection, but periodically yell at a child or at the whole group.

14. Make everyone do homework before they can have "play time."

15. Have no rules at all and no planned activities either.

16. Keep children in groups selected by the staff with little opportunity for spending time with friends in other groups.

17. Have a tightly controlled schedule in which children move from one planned enrichment activity to another with no opportunity for "just hanging out."

18. Keep all art materials in a teachers' storage cabinet with children required to ask every time they want something.

➤ Did you think of some ideas that were not on the list? This list, of course, could go on much longer.

No matter how many more ingenious and mischievous ideas we might add, we would find that each of them would fall under one or more of the *six key elements of a school-age care program.*

Six Key Elements of a School-Age Care Program

Program Element #1
Children's basic needs: recognition, attention, freedom from fear, autonomy and food

Program Element #2
Physical environment: traffic patterns, room arrangements, furnishings and the way space is set up

Program Element #3
Activities and schedules: what is taking place and the duration and sequence in which it is taking place

Program Element #4
Social groupings: the size and composition of groupings and how the groups are formed

Program Element #5
Rules: the way expectations for appropriate behavior are communicated (or not communicated)

Program Element #6
Consequences: the way positive behaviors and undesired behaviors are (or are not) reinforced

Do Behavior Problems "Live" In The Children?

What can we learn about children's behavior and misbehavior in SAC settings by coming in, as we have just done, "through the back door"? The exercise in which we just engaged teaches us that each time we set up a room, make and enforce rules, choose an activity, divide children into groups or plan a snack, we have the power to generate lots of misbehavior. We, therefore, have enormous power over the behavior of children, because it is not the children who have primary responsibility to make decisions regarding these basic program elements -- it is we, the staff. If our decisions and actions can contribute to *mis*behavior, then our decisions and actions can also contribute to appropriate behavior.

Do behavior problems, then, "live" inside the children? Do the problems enter the room when certain "difficult" children walk in? Most of the time the answer is "no." Most problems "live" in the environment that we create. We have the power to generate the problems, and we have the power to minimize them. An intelligent gardener who finds her plot overrun with weeds questions her gardening techniques and seldom is heard blaming the stunted vegetables. An intelligent caregiver in school-age care adopts a similar outlook toward the management of behavior and misbehavior.

Prevention or Treatment?
Examining the Six Key Elements
in Your Program

The concept of treatment is associated with the practice of medicine, while the concept of prevention is associated with public health. Which makes more sense: to continue to treat individual patients displaying the symptoms of typhus bacteria (the treatment approach) or to identify the source of raw sewage seeping into the town water supply and correct it (the prevention approach)? Most people would readily agree that, in this example, the prevention approach is both more intelligent and more cost-effective. Yet, when it comes to managing misbehavior, unfortunately, caregivers in SAC (and parents, too) frequently resort to the treatment approach: what should we do about Gregory's behavior? How can we crack down harder on that group of fourth grade girls? What clever consequences can we think up if Randi pulls that stunt again?

Think about it. You have only so much physical, emotional and mental energy to invest in responding to behavior problems. Do you want to invest that energy in taking measures to reduce the chances of behavior problems or do you prefer to wait for the problems to arise and then "treat" them? If you choose the prevention approach, then begin by examining the basic program elements we have identified and consider how your program design stands up in each area. In particular, you begin with *the first four elements*. The last two elements - devising of rules and consequences - are too often the first aspects of behavior management people think about. They should come, however, only after you have looked carefully at the first four.

1.) Children's Basic Needs

All the motivation in the world will not make a disciple out of a child whose basic needs are denied or overlooked. How well does your program address these needs? The first and most basic need is for **recognition**. Are children greeted warmly by name on arrival each day? Do they have a private space to keep their belongings?

Children also need **attention**. Is there an opportunity for individual attention and interaction with them over the course of the time in the SAC setting?

They need to be **free of fear**. Are you -- knowingly or unknowingly -- allowing older or more dominant children to threaten or abuse younger or less confident children? What about fears that children bring with them from outside the setting, e.g. the fear that the parents will forget "whose turn it is to pick me up"? Is there space and time in your program for these fears to be addressed and calmed?

They also need **autonomy**. That means their independence must be recognized, in accordance with their particular age and developmental level. Making them dependent on you for toys and games, art materials, snacks, permission to go to the bathroom, etc., runs counter to their basic needs and will sooner or later foster misbehavior.

Eating and **autonomy over one's own food** intake is a basic need of school-agers. Many are ravenous after spending the day in a classroom. Most children will stop when they have eaten enough and will still have an appetite for supper later on. Strict limits on snack consumption set by staff should be the exception, not the rule, in SAC programs.

2.) Physical Environment

Is your SAC program an attractive, inviting space to enter? If it is a shared space, do you simply leave all the tables and chairs where they were (to avoid the hassle of putting them back later) or do you rearrange the room to make it more conducive to school-age care? (Remember, if you do need to move things around, the children may enjoy helping with that.) Have you included soft chairs or pillows to make it less institutional and more home-like? Is the space set up and divided in such a way that it is clear where different activities belong (block building, table games, arts/crafts, books, music, dress-up and house-keeping)? Walls or large partitions are not needed to divide space: tape lines on the floor, small area rugs and movable storage cabinets do very nicely.

3.) Activities and Schedules

Do your activities reflect a wide range of interests, from artistic expression to food preparation to the need for peer interaction to vigorous physical activity such as sports, dance and martial arts? Do the activities respond to specific interests expressed by the children? How does your schedule account for the differing attention spans of kindergartners, as opposed to fourth or fifth graders? Is the schedule an endless series of "one-shot" activities or do you have ongoing activities such as drama groups - where children work on a play or dance performance - or clubs, where children pursue common ongoing interests? Do you introduce new activities frequently so that the older children don't feel like they've "seen it all before"?

4.) Social Groupings

How much time is spent in a large group and how much in smaller groupings? Are smaller groupings based on age/grade level, on interest in a particular activity or some other criterion? Are children kept in the same small groups consistently or do they change? Are they assigned by staff or do they choose? Is there an opportunity for children to opt out of planned groupings and do something alone or with one or two friends? There isn't any one "best practice" in the formation of social groupings. It is healthy to experiment with different arrangements and to monitor the opinions of the children -- and the effect on behavior.

5.) Rules

Rules will be discussed after we have examined the first four elements.

6.) Consequences

Consequences are discussed in conjunction with rules in the next section of this book.

Identifying Patterns and Reducing Behavior Problems

Let us suppose you and other members of your SAC staff have taken a prevention approach and designed the basic elements of your program in such a way as to meet the needs of children and reduce the likelihood of behavior problems. Are you finished dealing with behavior problems? Not likely! However, your thoughts about your program are now organized in such a way that it will be easy for you to identify where you need to make changes.

When you see children behaving in inappropriate ways, ask yourself the following series of questions regarding the basic elements of your program:

What basic needs of the children, such as hunger, the need to be physically active or their need for autonomy and recognition, might be at the root of their behavior? Do we need to find better ways to acknowledge and address **the children's basic needs**?

Where did it take place? Do we need to rearrange the **physical environment**?

When did it take place? Do we need to adjust our **activity** choices or the way this particular activity is conducted? Do we need to rethink the way we have set up our **schedule**?

With whom did it take place? Do we need to alter the composition of our **social groupings** or figure out a new plan for how the children are divided into groups for activities?

The following examples illustrate how this approach works in practice.

"The Transition Time From Hell"

At John Raditz Extended Day Care, the adult-directed activity period began after snack time. Somehow, the transition time from snack to the activities just seemed to get worse every day. The 45 children sat at any of three long tables in the school cafeteria. Before snack was served, they listened to the staff announce the upcoming activities. After that, snack would be served, with the three staff members each supervising one of the tables. As soon as all the children at one table were finished, that staff member would proceed to set up his or her activity, announcing, for instance, "OK, the mask-making activity will be starting in Room 5." Children from that table who were doing the mask-making would accompany that staff person, but the others would be left behind without supervision. By the time the second staff member's table was ready to go, some of the children from the first table managed to get themselves in trouble. By the time the third table full of children was ready, the one remaining adult had several children on "time out" and had yelled herself hoarse trying to keep control of the situation.

13

One member of the staff thought they should wait until everyone at all the snack tables was finished before starting the activities. Others didn't like that idea. What could they do? They looked at the problem using the framework described previously:

What basic needs of the children might be at the root of their behavior?
It didn't seem to be related to needs not being met.

Where did it take place?
In the cafeteria.

When did it take place?
Around 3:15 p.m., as snack time was ending and activity time was getting ready to start.

With whom did it take place?
The behavior problems did not come from any one age group. The boys and girls of any age seated at the unattended snack tables seemed to start bouncing off the walls.

A quick discussion among the staff revealed that no one thought any of the **children's basic needs** were being overlooked or that the set-up of the **physical environment** of the cafeteria itself was the problem. Some would have liked to eliminate the **activity,** because it had become such an awful time but, after all, there had to be a snack time and, therefore, there had to be a transition from snack time. No one thought that putting snack at a different time on the **schedule** would clear up the problem, either. That left the **social groupings** to think about: was there some way to reorganize their composition? Yes! A few minutes of brainstorming brought the following agreement: after each staff member announced his or her upcoming activity, children would move (if they weren't already sitting there) to the snack table supervised by that adult whose activity they planned to join. That would create a disruption for a minute or two, but once everyone was re-seated, each group could take as long as they needed for snack and move at their own pace into the activity period.

After the change was made, the staff could not believe how much energy they had been wasting every day "disciplining" the children who misbehaved during the transition period, and how little time it had actually taken to analyze and solve the problem. They realized that, for a long time, they had blamed and punished children for behavior problems that were actually caused by their own program design.

Solutions:

- Before serving snack, the teachers announce the activity choices -- as in the past.
- Children get up and move to the table where the staff member leading their preferred activity is stationed (or stay where they are if they are already with that person).

"Multiple Bus Routes, Multiple Trouble"

At Jose Marti SAC, children arrived over a 30 minute period from several different schools. Children who arrived early had time for free play. All activities were put away and snack served as soon as the last bus arrived. However, sometimes the last bus was delayed. Early arrivals, who were anxiously awaiting their snack, often misbehaved. Other times the misbehavior came from those who arrived on the last bus -- in particular, a group of older girls who insisted they wanted to have free play time before settling down for snack. The trouble also came from a few of their girl friends who wanted to "hang out" with them and who had already arrived earlier.

The staff looked at the problem using the framework mentioned:

What basic needs of the children might be at the root of their behavior?
Some children were getting overly hungry. We may also be failing to acknowledge and address the older kids' need for "peer relations."

Where did it take place?
In the cafeteria, and sometimes in the activity room, where the girls would continue to disrupt after snack.

When did it take place?
Free play before snack, snack time and the activity following.

With whom did it take place?
First group to arrive, last group to arrive, worst problem with older girls.

Discussion among the staff focused on all four possible points of adjustment. All agreed that starting snack earlier was a good idea, because most children really were hungry when they arrived. One staff member thought the older girls were just deliberately "being brats," but eventually even she agreed that it was worth considering that their social needs were being underestimated. There was some interest in subdividing the cafeteria space so one area would be set aside for snack, while activities could go on simultaneously in another area. (This could also be viewed as a redefining of the type of activity and a change in the schedule.) It would also bring about a change in social groupings, since snack would no longer be a large group activity.

It took a few weeks to work out the new system satisfactorily. Under the new system, children from the first group began setting up snack almost as soon as they had arrived. Children rotated as "snack helpers." The staff made it clear that, without children's assistance in setting up and cleaning up, they would have to return to the old procedure. "Snack helpers" from the last group had snack completely put away 20 minutes after they arrived. The girls on the last bus could "hang out" for 10 minutes and then have snack. In the end, both staff and children were much happier with the new procedure, and behavior problems were dramatically reduced. The staff of this program also realized that they had been blaming the children -- and scapegoating the group of older girls -- for problems that were generated by their own lack of careful planning.

Solutions:

- Begin serving snack as soon as the first group arrives.
- Utilize school-agers as "snack-helpers" with the set-up and clean-up.
- Allow older girls a chance to socialize.

When caregivers think about **behavior management** and **discipline,** they often think first about rules and how to deal with those who break them. But the two illustrations just given demonstrate that **rules** and **consequences** are not the caregivers' first line of defense when they observe problems. We should always begin with questions about those **four basic program elements:** *children's basic needs, physical environment, activities and schedule, social groupings.*

18

Control The Climate, Not The Children

Starting with questions about whether we are addressing the basic needs of children and about the appropriateness of our use of physical space, our activities, our schedule and our social groupings sets a very positive tone for a program. What it communicates is that we are trying to develop a climate that is healthy for children and that is responsive to their needs. To begin with rules and a list of consequences (or *punishments*) that result for those who break the rules sets a very different tone. The first message says, "I am trying to control the climate and I trust that the vast majority of children will respond positively to a healthy climate." The second message says, "I am trying to control the children. I do not trust children to be naturally responsive and cooperative, but I believe that with enough rules and enough consequences we can keep everything under control." Which message do you prefer to send?

Rules and Consequences

It would be useless to focus on rules and appropriate behavior without first addressing children's basic needs and carefully planning your physical space, activities, schedule and social groupings. Nevertheless, once you have invested time and thought into these program elements you will need to develop an understanding of cx pectations for appropriate behavior and communicate these expectations to participants in your SAC program. How do you do this?

19

Communicating Expectations
About Appropriate Behavior

Be concise and be positive

Rules stated simply are easier to learn and remember, rules stated positively set a better climate. Which sounds better to you: "Respect other people's private space and property" or "Keep your hands on your own body, and stay out of other people's cubbies"?

Put rules in writing and post them prominently

Important rules which need to be frequently invoked should be neatly printed and posted in a place that allows staff and children to easily refer to them. Of course, children who do not read will need to have them explained orally. This is a good demonstration to young children of the power and importance of written communication.

Ask parents to assist in clarifying important rules

Some SAC programs send home a copy of the rules, others go a step further and turn a list of important rules into a written contract between the child and the program. They send two copies of the contract home with the child and ask the parents to read it over and discuss it with the children. The children then sign one copy and return it to the program, keeping the other copy for themselves and their families.

Make only rules the staff plans to respect!

How many times does it happen? The rule says "We sit on chairs, we use tables for games and activities." But the staff member sits on the table! The message to children is that "might makes right," rules have no intrinsic value and it's fine to break rules if you can get away with it.

Be sure discussion of rules in a large group is only the beginning

Do you rely exclusively on **large group** discussions of important rules and behavioral issues? Some children "tune out" during large group discussions and will miss everything you say. You may take the attitude "well, if they can't listen, that's *their* problem." Or you may recognize that we all have different learning styles. If you take the latter approach, you will find opportunities to explain the rules in **small groups** or even **individually** for those children who don't concentrate well in a group.

Do you rely on discussions held at the beginning of the year and after that it's, "Hey, you know the rules! We went over this in September!" Many children have a lot on their minds in September -- new school classrooms, new friends, new after-school arrangements. They need many more opportunities to become familiar with your expectations.

Clarify expectations immediately prior to specific activities

It would be unrealistic to explain the rules of the gym while you are in the cafeteria and expect all the children, once they actually get into the gym, to remember all the rules and comply with them. Instead, sit down inside the gym and discuss behavioral expectations prior to beginning the play or activity period. Do this, not just once, but the first several times you bring your group into the gym -- or into any other space that is new to them.

When you are introducing unfamiliar craft materials, a new game or any other new activity, follow a similar pattern. Make sure children have a chance to understand your expectations before they "get themselves in trouble" by using the material or playing the game in a way that you regard as inappropriate.

Provide individual guidance for individual children

You will become familiar over time with the behavior patterns of individual children. Since you are more interested in "prevention" than "treatment," you will want to devise your own strategies for helping individual children avoid misbehaving. There is nothing wrong with calling Terry aside at the start of the outdoor play period (out of earshot of the other children) and saying "Terry, remember what happened yesterday in the sand box? I want you to have a good time today and not have problems out here, so why don't you repeat to me the rules for the sand box area?" To follow up, you may want to seek out Terry a few minutes later, ask how things are going, put your hand on his shoulder, let him know he is doing fine. You will always find prevention less costly than treatment -- in your time, energy and morale!

Rewarding and Reinforcing Desired Behavior

Informal reinforcement

Do you pay attention, express appreciation, show a personal interest and offer affection to children who are meeting your expectations? Or is it easier to get a caregiver's time and attention in your SAC program by breaking a rule? Children will quickly get the message if good behavior gets ignored while improper behavior gets attention. Some children will continue behaving properly but will feel discouraged while others will turn to disruption or aggression because they crave personal recognition and attention -- even if it must be of the negative kind.

Informal reinforcement of appropriate behavior begins simply by greeting children as they arrive, asking them how they feel or how things went in school that day. It continues through all activities and routines: do staff sit among children and carry on brief conversations during free play time, outdoor play time or snack time? Or do they seem to prefer congregating and talking to each other -- until "trouble" breaks out?

One ingenious method for reinforcing positive behavior is to occasionally leave handwritten notes for children in their cubbies. A simple sentence such as "It was fun having you in my cooking group today. See you soon!" requires about 30 seconds to write. Children love to receive such notes. They can be especially meaningful to children with histories of difficult behavior. These children are used to having notes sent home from teachers-- but written only to the parents and seldom very flattering. It is also a good idea to have staff mailboxes where children can deliver mail (notes or art work) to caregivers. Write a warm, friendly note to that "angry, difficult child," and you may be shocked at the expressions of love and appreciation that come back to you.

Be persistent in reinforcing positive behavior, and do not expect quick turnarounds in the behavior of those who have presented many problems. Keep in mind that some children have had many years of training, both in their families and in school, that positive behavior goes unnoticed -- or can leave you exposed and vulnerable -- while negative behavior draws attention. By age eight or so, many children disguise their positive feelings under a veneer of sarcasm or "machismo." You have to learn to "read" the signals. The caption on the picture a child leaves in your mailbox may say "This ugly face is *you!*" but the unspoken message is " I took the time to draw this just for you."

What about formal rewards, incentives, positive reinforcement?

School-age children do like and respond to formal recognition and rewards, but such schemes should occur very soon after the behavior being rewarded and be logically related to the behavior. Offering a field trip to a museum as a reward for children who avoid fist-fighting for a week makes little logical sense. However, offering a field trip to look at Japanese horticulture to children involved in a nature and gardening project is quite sensible — and would likely motivate a few children to get more involved in the project. On the other hand, if you really want everyone to go on that field trip, do not hold it out as a reward; simply plan it as an activity in which everyone will participate.

Point systems — in which children accumulate (or lose) points for behavior in a variety of different situations, and then receive an *unrelated* reward at the end of the week or the month — do very little to help children improve behavior and waste the time of caregivers who have to keep track of such schemes. On the other hand, some programs have successfully influenced children toward more positive behavior with certificates that are **logically related** to exemplary behavior -- for instance, "good sportsmanship," "safety awareness," or "leadership." These can be handed out once a week during snack time or large group time accompanied by a drum roll, a song or some kind of school-age "pomp and circumstance."

Of course you want to avoid any formal reward systems which only tend to reinforce the self-esteem of the children who already feel good about themselves and overlook the other children. It is important, too, that you do not find yourselves simply rewarding the most passive and compliant children. There is little point in using formal rewards at all unless you can find creative ways to recognize the positive contributions of the children who tend to have lower self-esteem and who are more likely to present behavior problems.

Involve children in setting rules and consequences

Some programs pretend to be democracies and begin each year with a completely blank slate of rules, implying that the only rules will be the ones drawn up by the children. In reality, certain rules are fundamental to the philosophy of the program, and staff consciously steer the children to "reinvent" these rules each year. For instance, "We use words, not violence, to solve problems" or "We respect other people's color, nationality and sex".

If certain rules (such as the above) do reflect ongoing program values and philosophy there is no reason why you have to start with a blank slate. It is better to start with those rules intact. There are still lots of areas for children to be involved in rule-making. In fact, they'll be much more interested in formulating rules that govern more specific aspects of the program. For instance, you want to have an area set aside for homework. What part of the room (or what room) will be designated for that purpose? How should the area be set up? Will talking be allowed? Studying together? What should be the consequences of using the area inappropriately or disrupting those who are trying to study? What if children want to use the area for something other than homework, if no one is doing homework?

Or suppose you want to have a club for fifth and sixth graders but the only space for it is a room currently used for art projects or showing videos. How can you accomplish both purposes? Let the fifth and sixth graders have it two days a week and leave it for art and videos the other three days? Which days? When it is used by the fifth and sixth graders will any younger children be allowed in? What consequences will be established for improper use of the room?

Given a chance to hold some discussions, SAC programs often find that children develop more intelligent and workable solutions regarding such nitty-gritty matters than the staff ever could.

Look for natural and logical consequences and avoid unrelated consequences

When children fail to meet your expectations for appropriate behavior, what are the consequences? Are they logically related to the misbehavior -- or completely unrelated? Students of child development agree that children learn best from **natural consequences**, i.e., consequences that flow directly from the behavior without any need for intervention by the caregiver. A classic illustration of this principle is the child who puts her hand too close to a hot flame; there is an immediate, tangible, painful consequence that effectively teaches the child to be wary of getting too close to such a flame in the future.

An example of the principle of **natural consequence**s in the SAC setting is the child who cheats when playing board games and then finds other children declining his invitations to play such games. It may be useful in such a circumstance for a staff member to discuss the problem with the child but not to apply additional consequences. The natural consequences, all by themselves, teach the child a very powerful lesson.

In situations where no natural consequences seem to flow directly from the behavior, staff need to devise **logical consequences**. Examples include: telling a child who is careless in the use of games or toys that she may only use certain games or toys under direct adult supervision, or telling the child who fails to follow directions during a field trip that she will not be included on a future trip until she can make a commitment to better behavior. It is important to note the difference between **logical consequences** and *punishment*. If you present consequences as punishment, designed to "show the child who's boss," you are only teaching that you have the capacity to assert your authority over the child. But consequences logically related to the misbehavior and presented in a non-punitive manner teach the child about appropriate and inappropriate behavior.

Too often, the consequences that are used by adults trying to influence children's behavior are presented as punishment and are completely unrelated to the behaviors themselves. Unrelated consequences do little to guide children toward appropriate behavior the next time they face a similar situation. When children receive punishment ,they are encouraged to feel bad about themselves. This in turn interferes with their development of a trusting relationship with you. But in order to become your disciples, they need to trust you. It is critical to find ways to provide limits and guidance without resorting to punitive methods and attitudes.

Value the child even when you don't accept or approve of the behavior

Use language carefully, and make clear to children that you can disapprove of behavior without disapproving of the person. "I like having you in my group, Shelly, but I don't like it when you . . . ." "You have really been irritating me today, Aletha, but I'm sure you'll come back tomorrow with your sweet disposition restored." If you have asked a child to sit and discuss a behavior problem with you or removed the child temporarily from an activity, do not leave the child with feelings of rejection. Bring it to closure -- it only takes a few seconds: "OK, Nigel. Have you thought about what happened between you and Farrell? Good -- now get back in there and enjoy yourself."

I Like You But Not Your Behavior!

- "I like having you in my group, Shelly, but I don't like it when you . . ."

- "OK, Nigel, have you thought about what happened between you and Farrell? Good -- now get back in there and enjoy yourself."

- "Remember how much fun we had together when . . .?"

- "If I turn around three times and click my heels together, will I find the Ashley that treats other people with respect, instead of the one that calls people names?"

- "Is this behavior working for you? Because it isn't working for me at all!"

- "I don't know why you are acting this way, but I know that there's a guy inside you who knows how to have better control over himself. And I'll be happy when he shows up again!"

- "Did you wake up on the wrong side of the bed today?"

- "Are you hungry or something? Didn't get enough rest last night? Got in trouble with your teacher? Because I know there's a reason for your behavior!"

Techniques to enhance the self-esteem of the "difficult" child

Children who repeatedly get themselves into trouble often have received a great deal of negative feedback from adults and do not think very highly of themselves. They may also have a hard time making friends. How can you set limits with such children and, at the same time, help them feel better about themselves? All of the following techniques are useful:

- Be on the lookout for times when the child is behaving appropriately and show a personal interest.

- Have a staff member posted to watch for the child to arrive at the program and prepared to provide one-on-one attention for the first few minutes. Sometimes a good start will carry over to the rest of the afternoon. (So will a bad start.)

- Let the child be the first to learn to use a new game or toy, and then introduce it to others.

- Include the child in a small group activity in which you have hand-picked children who are likely to be accepting of him/her.

- Increase the number of mixed-age activities. Children who are unpopular within their own peer group may do much better if mixed in with older or younger children.

Promote problem-solving and conflict resolution, avoid blaming and shaming

What is your first response when you witness aggressive behavior or a serious conflict among children? Caregivers often turn first to the child who seemed to be the aggressor, reprimand him or her, and demand that an apology be made to the other child. After that, they turn their attention to comforting the "victimized" child -- who may have continued to let the tears run profusely while the caregiver spoke to the "offender." (Did you ever notice how quickly some children "turn off" the tears once it is their turn to talk?) Let us look briefly at the messages that are communicated when we follow that procedure.

Message #1: There is a "good guy" and a "bad guy" in a conflict situation.

Message #2: The "bad guy" (the "aggressor") must be more important than the "good guy" (the "victim") since that's who gets our attention first.

Message #3: We -- the adults -- are in charge of resolving conflicts among children.

Message #4: The way we resolve conflicts is to encourage children to lie about their feelings (say you're "sorry" whether you really feel that way or not).

Are these really the messages we wish to be sending to children? It would seem to be far more sensible to break this pattern and change all four of the messages.

31

How about the following?:

Message #1: Conflicts are a part of group living, whether in families, classrooms or anywhere else. They don't happen because somebody is a "bad guy."

Message #2: We treat all parties involved with equal respect and sympathy. Our first concern is with the physical safety of all members of our group, so we give first attention to anyone who is physically hurt.

Message #3: Everyone, adults *and* children, participates in conflict resolution -- preferably after the sobbing has ended and we are ready to calm down and think about it. This conflict has already occurred. Can we learn something about how it happened so it will be less likely to occur next time?

Message #4: We encourage an airing of honest opinions and feelings by those involved. An apology is one possible resolution -- but only if it is sincerely offered.

How can we send this second set of messages instead of the first set? When we encounter a conflict situation, we can first check to see if anyone was hurt and provide first aid and comfort to anyone who is -- regardless of "who started it." We can then encourage a calm discussion of what happened -- with the emphasis on identifying what choices participants in the conflict made that escalated the conflict and what *different* choices in a future situation could avoid such escalation. Once having arrived at some information that may be useful in a similar situation in the future, we can ask the participants how they want to bring this one to an end. They may want to shake hands. One of them may want to apologize. One may want to invite the other to resume playing together. Or they may prefer to go off in separate directions. We caregivers can endorse any one of these endings and wish them well.

Caregivers get frustrated and upset too -- how do you handle it?

Staff in school-age care need to know that getting aggravated with children at times is a normal reaction. Taking out that aggravation on children, however, is unacceptable. What do you do to keep from going "over the edge"? First, learn to monitor yourself for signals. Sometimes the aggravation level will reveal itself through your body language or tone of voice, even though you are still mouthing all the appropriate words. Or you might notice that you've lost your sense of humor -- the children are laughing and you aren't.

Once you've read your own signals, you need to find a way to release some tension. Slow, deep breathing while counting to ten is a classic technique. Or, if there are enough staff, you may be able to take an unscheduled break. A three or four minute walk away from the area can be very helpful. (You have to let other staff members know where you are, of course.) If you can't leave the area, you might try simply acknowledging to the children you are supervising that you've reached the "burn-out" point. "Don't talk to me for a minute. I'm closing my eyes and skiing down a mountain in Colorado." If you are the uninhibited type you can say, "Pardon me, but I feel the need for a little scream" and then do it! Almost anything you do at this point will get you back to a more balanced frame of mind. The most important step is recognizing when you've reached that point of extreme frustration.

Children With Disabilities and Special Needs

Everything discussed in this book applies to children with special needs. To gain their trust and cultivate them as potential disciples, you need to be sure you are not overlooking any of their basic needs. Does the physical environment need to be adjusted in any way to accommodate them? (Is the room arranged so a child in a wheelchair is able to maneuver?) Are the activities, schedule and social groupings suitable? (Children with limited speech and language, as well as children with emotional and behavioral problems, may do much better in smaller groupings.)

Will children with special needs understand the rules and the consequences of breaking the rules? Those who are hearing-impaired need to receive information through visual and other means. Those who are visually-impaired need to receive information auditorally. Those who are mentally retarded or developmentally delayed may need things explained at their own level. But you are already prepared for this. You have made plans to share information about rules and appropriate behavior with all children in a variety of ways -- orally, in writing, large groups, small groups and individually. You will do this throughout the year, not just in September. You're even asking the parents to help familiarize their children with appropriate behavior in your program.

Some children, however, will not respond well to your efforts to encourage appropriate behavior because they have emotional, learning or developmental problems that interfere with their ability to do so. Once you recognize that a child's challenging behaviors are related to a learning or emotional condition, how do you handle it?

Here are some ideas to consider when working with children with disablities and special needs:

- Find out more about the child's condition. Invite someone with expertise -- the child's parent, a school psychologist, etc. -- to attend a staff meeting.

- If the child you are working with is not a special education student, find out what the referral procedure is for getting him or her formally evaluated. Someone will have to be in communication with the child's school in order to find this out and to find out why it has not taken place before. (Are they observing similar behaviors, learning or communication problems?)

- Ignore some of the behaviors. You might allow a child to wander while others are sitting, or touch other children's hair even though they are supposed to "keep their hands to themselves." You may also allow "partial participation" in activities, i.e., the child participates in his/her own way.

- Change some of the rules. A child with mental retardation or autism might benefit from bringing a small toy to the snack table, even though other children are not allowed to do so. Or you might change the rules for everyone. You might decide that bringing a small, unobtrusive toy to the snack table would actually allow everyone to have a more peaceful and fun snack time.

Parents and Families as Your Allies

Earlier, we discussed making copies of important rules available to families and enlisting their help in clarifying expectations for children. But parents can help in many other ways as well. Ask them, as part of the enrollment process, to identify particular interests and hobbies of their children. By incorporating some of these into your activity plans, you will appeal to children's interests and reduce the potential for boredom and the resulting misbehavior. Ask parents to keep you informed when changes are taking place in their children's lives that may be reflected in behavior. (Among these would be changes in where they live or in who is living with them.) Demonstrate an ongoing interest in getting to know parents and how they are doing in their home lives and work lives. Do not give the impression that your interest is confined only to the times when their children exhibit behavior problems.

It is especially important to develop good communication with the parents of children whose behavior poses the most problems for you. These parents may sometimes seem difficult to speak with and defensive -- particularly if, in the past, teachers have made them feel their children's behavior was a reflection of their own character or lack of parenting ability. Part of your job is to put parents at ease and assure them that you are not blaming them for their children's behavior problems. Rather, you want to work with them as allies with the common goal of helping the child be a successful participant in your program.

Much communication with families can take place informally. However, you may also want to conduct formal staff-parent conferences. (Some programs convene staff-child-parent conferences, in which children attend part of the meeting and contribute to the discussion of how to improve their participation in the program.) A cardinal rule in such a conference is to always begin by reporting on the positive points of children's participation. "Everyone on our staff has enjoyed getting to know Caleb. He is a very creative spirit..." Another cardinal rule is to do your homework before the conference. Do not make vague comments about "poor behavior" or "lack of cooperation." Be prepared with specific illustrations of the misbehavior that concerns you. Avoid clinical terms or labels such as "aggressive" or "disturbed" or "hyperactive," and stick with the facts as you have observed them. Have in mind one or two priority behaviors that need to be worked on and improved now. If there are more, save them for a future conference. Always set a date for follow-up communication (over the phone or in person) before you bring the discussion to an end.

In the case of a child whose behaviors include some that cannot be tolerated, such as threatening and violent behavior towards staff or children or attempts to leave supervised areas without permission, a conference should produce a contract with a very clear and strong commitment by the child to change these behaviors within a specific short-term timetable. In the event these behaviors persist, a tentative date for termination of the child's enrollment should be indicated.

Contracts are also a good idea for helping children work on behaviors which may not be quite so serious. One child in a SAC program agreed she was whining too much and that staff mark on a chart each time she "whined or complained." After seven times in any one day she would stop. Believe it or not, she *did* stop. School-age children enjoy having contracts printed up and signed. It makes them feel important -- and helps them work on changing their behavior.

Communication with School Personnel

Staff in SAC settings may or may not see the same kinds of behavior problems as teachers in school classrooms. Because of the difference in structure, curriculum and goals in the two settings, some children who have behavior problems in school do quite nicely in SAC. Others, who may thrive in the structure of the school classroom, have more difficulty in SAC. To gain insights into a child's behavior patterns, it is best to have ongoing communication between those working in the SAC program and those working in the school or schools served by your program.

If your program is operated by the school district itself, then it should be relatively easy to establish channels of communication. The principal's office is usually the place to begin to open these channels. If the main purpose of the communication is to address behavior issues, the principal may choose to have someone from the counseling or school social work staff take a leadership role in facilitating contact with individual teachers.

If your program is independent of the school district, you will need permission from families to hold discussions with school personnel regarding the children you serve. It is recommended that at the time of enrollment you ask parents to sign permission slips for this communication. A simple statement such as the following is acceptable to the vast majority of parents:

Child's name: _____
School: _____
Grade: _____
Teacher's name: _____

From time to time we find it useful to speak with classroom teachers and other personnel from the school attended by your child. With your permission, we will carry out such communication only for the benefit of your child. (For instance, if we are trying to get ideas to help your child improve his/her behavior.) Any information obtained in the course of this communication will be treated as strictly confidential.

For the school year beginning in August 19__ I grant permission for the type of communication described above to take place.

_____   _____
Parent signature   Date

It is better to gain such permission from all families at the time of enrollment than to wait until the need to communicate with the school arises. Once a problem has arisen, some parents may become defensive and less inclined to authorize the communication. On the other hand, most parents see communication between the two organizations as proper and professional and will be glad to know that school and the SAC program are working together to help their child.

Once you have permission for the communication, you have access to an important resource. Classroom teachers have been known to telephone SAC programs before the end of the afternoon saying, "Jason had a really terrible day today and tried to run away from school." That's the day you want to be sure and post a staff member to watch for Jason and try to help him avoid trouble from the moment he arrives. The SAC program and the school can also share with each other activities or behavior management techniques that seem to help Jason.

Putting Your Discipline and Termination Policies in Writing

Families -- and the school-agers, too -- are entitled to know what steps your program will take in the event that a child continues to engage in problematic behaviors. Your parent handbook should clearly spell out the kinds of behaviors that are considered to pose serious problems, and include the steps and procedures leading up to, and resulting in termination.

You will want to indicate that your response to behavior problems includes all of the approaches discussed in this book:

1. Assessment of the program to see if any of the **child's basic needs** are being overlooked

2. Assessment of the **physical environment**, the **activities and schedule** and the **social groupings** to see if any of them can be adapted to help improve the child's behavior

3. Assessment of the way **expectations** (rules) are being explained and the types of **consequences** that are being offered for both appropriate and inappropriate behavior

4. Ongoing informal **communication** with **families** and *at least* one formal conference seeking their help in moving the child toward successful participation

5. **Communication** with **school personnel** (if permitted by the family) seeking their ideas to help solve the child's behavior problems

41

6. A **contract** addressing specific behaviors and their specific timetables, indicating that failure will lead to termination by a specific date

7. Termination, in the event none of these strategies are successful (some programs build in a suspension for several days prior to termination)

In the event a participant in your program meets the definition of a "person with a disability" as defined in the Americans with Disabilities Act of 1990, you will have to document that you made all reasonable and readily-achievable accommodations and program modifications prior to discontinuing services to the child or youth. Moreover, you must document that the denial of continued services was in no way an act of discrimination. That is, under the same or similar circumstances, a participant without a disability would also have been terminated from the program. (Any student currently or previously receiving special education services is a "person with a disability" under the ADA. There are others, however, who never received special education services but may also be classified as "persons with a disability.")

Conclusion

The secret committee to which Tracy Kidder referred (in the quotation on page 1) may or may not continue to influence the classrooms of our nation, but those of us working with children and youth before and after school owe it no allegiance at all. The truth is, we will find most boys and girls much more compliant (and a lot more fun to be around) if we stop trying to control their behavior and start trying to control the climates of our programs. Viewing parents as our allies and cultivating good communication with them is one part of that positive climate; developing relationships with school staff and other community agencies is another. Remember that, in the vast majority of cases, behavior problems live in the environment -- in the way we set up our space, select our activities and form our social groupings -- not in the children. The power to generate behavior problems -- or to keep them to a minimum -- is in the hands of the caregiving staff.

To uplift the self-esteem of the most difficult children is not easy, since the attitudes they adopt are based on a number of years of life experience. Yet each time we go out of our way to let them know that we like them — and that we are capable of making a distinction between the behavior that is unacceptable and the human being who is acceptable and likable — we have a chance of reawakening those buried feelings of self-worth. The words and gestures required to reach out to children in that fashion take only a few minutes, yet spread out across days, weeks or months. The pride felt by any caregiver who succeeds in turning a "discipline problem" into a disciple lasts a lifetime.

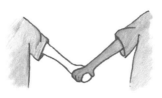

For Further Reading

School-Age NOTES (monthly newsletter)
P.O. Box 40205
Nashville TN 37204
Phone: 800-410-8780/615-279-0700
www.afterschoolcatalog.com

Adventures in Peacemaking:
A Conflict Resolution Activity Guide
for School-Age Programs
William Kreidler & Lisa Furlong (1996), ESR
Available from School-Age NOTES

Creative Conflict Resolution: More Than 200
Activities for Keeping Peace in the Classroom
William Kreidler (1984), Good Year Books
Available from School-Age NOTES

Half A Childhood: Quality Programs for
Out-of-School Hours, 2nd Ed., Revised
Bender, et al (2000), School-Age NOTES

How To Talk So Kids Will Listen &
Listen So Kids Will Talk
Adele Faber & Elaine Mazlish (2002), Quill
Available from School-Age NOTES

How To Handle A Hard-To-Handle Kid
C. Drew Edwards, Ph.D. (1999), Free Spirit
Available from School-Age NOTES